What's Life Like in a Blended Family?

Grace Houser

PowerKiDS press.

NEW YORK

Published in 2019 by The Rosen Publishing Group, Inc.
29 East 21st Street, New York, NY 10010

First Edition

Editor: Greg Roza
Book Design: Rachel Rising

Photo Credits: Cover Ariel Skelley/DigitalVision/Getty Images; p. 5 pixelheadphoto digitalskillet/Shutterstock.com; p. 6 Hogan Imaging/Shutterstock.com; p. 7 ESB Professional/Shutterstock.com; p. 8 raluca teodorescu/Shutterstock.com; pp. 9, 19 Monkey Business Images/Shutterstock.com; p. 11 CandyBox Images/Shutterstock.com; p. 13 Trotskaya Nastassia/Shutterstock.com; p. 14 Matthias G. Ziegler/Shutterstock.com; p. 15 wavebreakmedia/Shutterstock.com; p. 17 sirtravelalot/Shutterstock.com; p. 18 Ruslan Guzov/Shutterstock.com; p. 21 michaeljung/Shutterstock.com; p. 22 Rob Marmion/Shutterstock.com.

Cataloging-in-Publication Data

Names: Houser, Grace.
Title: What's life like in a blended family? / Grace Houser.
Description: New York : PowerKids Press, 2019. | Series: Help me understand | Includes glossary and index.
Identifiers: ISBN 9781538348086 (pbk.) | ISBN 9781538348109 (library bound) | ISBN 9781538348093 (6pack)
Subjects: LCSH: Stepfamilies–Juvenile literature. | Divorce–Juvenile literature. | Children of divorced parents–Juvenile literature.
Classification: LCC HQ759.92 H74 2019 | DDC 306.874'7–dc23

Manufactured in the United States of America

CPSIA Compliance Information: Batch #CWPK19. For Further Information contact Rosen Publishing, New York, New York at 1-800-237-9932

Contents

Blended Together 4

Why? 6

In the Beginning 8

Stepparents 10

Brothers and Sisters 14

Back and Forth 16

New Things 18

Dealing with Feelings 20

Blending Can Be Good 22

Glossary 23

Index 24

Websites 24

Blended Together

You've probably heard the word "blend" before, but it might have been referring to something like a milkshake or smoothie. That's because this word means to combine, or mix together, into a new whole.

When two people get married and at least one has kids with a different parent already, this forms a blended family. It can be hard to get used to this kind of family if you're used to something different.

Living in a blended family can be difficult at first. With time, though, you might find that your new family is something special.

Why?

There are many reasons why blended families form. Sometimes people with kids get **divorced**. If one parent remarries, that forms a blended family. Sometimes both parents in a new marriage may have kids from earlier marriages. That means you'll have stepbrothers or stepsisters in addition to a new stepmother or stepfather.

Sometimes, one parent in a family dies. If the other parent remarries, that makes a blended family. The two adults who make a blended family might have new kids together, too.

If you have a single parent who gets married, that also makes a blended family.

In the Beginning

With any luck, you'll get a chance to get to know any new family members long before you become an actual blended family. Your parent will probably **introduce** you to the new person they're dating and you'll have a chance to talk to them and learn more about them. This might seem weird to you, but it's good to give them a chance. You might really like them! It might be nice to have more family members.

It's OK if you want to take it slow when meeting a new person in your parent's life. Just be **polite** and give them a chance to be friendly.

Stepparents

If your parent marries someone new, they'll be your stepmother or stepfather. You might be pleased, or you might be worried and a little unhappy. It's **normal** and OK to feel both!

You don't have to feel bad if it takes you a while to get used to the idea of living in a blended family. And you don't have to feel **disloyal** to either of your birth parents if you like your new stepparent.

If your parents are divorced, you might have hoped they would get back together someday. This is normal. It can be hard to lose this hope.

It's important to remember that a new stepparent doesn't take the place of the parents you already have. You might not feel the same way about a stepparent that you do about your birth parents. That's totally natural.

However, you do have to be polite and treat your stepparent with respect. If you're not **comfortable** calling them "mom" or "dad," maybe you can come up with a good name together. Many kids refer to their stepparent by their real first name.

Sometimes, if a marriage is the start of a blended family, parents will find a way for the kids to take part in the wedding. You're all part of a new family!

Brothers and Sisters

If your new stepparent has kids, your blended family will include stepbrothers and stepsisters. You'll probably get a chance to meet them before you all become a family. It's good to get to know them, and it's good for them to get to know you. You might have a lot in common!

You might be worried that new brothers and sisters may mean your parent will have less time for you. You and your parent can find ways to get time alone together.

If you didn't have brothers or sisters before, it may be more difficult to get used to a blended family. Everyone needs to try to make it work.

Back and Forth

If your birth parents are divorced, you might have to go back and forth from one family to another. If both of your parents remarry, you might even have two blended families.

It can feel very **confusing** and uncertain having two different homes and families. You might feel like you don't know where you belong. Remember that both families love you and want you to be comfortable. Talk to your parents if you're having problems.

You might have your own bedroom at each home or you might have to share. You can decide what things you'd like to keep at each place and what you'd like to take with you.

New Things

Even if you're still in the same home you've always lived in, things will be different in a blended family. Your stepparent might have new rules. Your family might have a new **schedule** because of the new family members. You might eat some new things for dinner because your new stepbrothers or stepsisters like them.

You might not like the changes. But remember that your new family members are going through changes too. You can work together to make things feel normal again.

Your blended family can start new **traditions**. Maybe you can find a new game or activity you all really like to do together.

HOME

Dealing with Feelings

Even if you like your new stepparent, it can be very hard to get used to a new life. There will be many changes. You'll have many feelings. Some might be good and some might be bad. You might feel like you have to choose one parent or family over the other or feel **jealous** of your stepbrothers or stepsisters.

This is normal. Make sure you talk to your parents, stepparent, or another trusted adult. They can help you deal with these feelings.

If something is really bothering you, it's important to talk about it. It may help you feel better.

⟶

Blending Can Be Good

Life in a blended family will be different. It will be hard at times. You might be worried that you'll lose your place in your birth parent's life. But if you make sure to talk to your parent and get to know your stepparent and stepbrothers and stepsisters, you might find that it's nice to have new family members and new traditions.

Blending things together often makes something new and exciting. This is also true for blended families.

Glossary

comfortable: Having no unpleasant feelings, worries, or uncertainty.

confusing: Hard to understand.

disloyal: Failing to support or be true to someone.

divorce: To stop being married to one another.

introduce: To make someone known to someone else.

jealous: Unhappy or angry because you feel someone else has something you want.

normal: Usual, not strange.

polite: Showing good manners and respect for others.

schedule: A list of times when certain events will happen.

tradition: A way of thinking, behaving, or doing something that's been used by people in a particular family for a long time.

Index

A

adult, 20

C

changes, 18, 20

F

feelings, 20

H

home, 16, 18
hope, 10

K

kids, 4, 6, 12, 14

M

marriage, 6, 12

N

names, 12

P

parent, 4, 6, 7, 8, 9, 10, 12,
        14, 16, 20, 22
problems, 16

R

respect, 12
rules, 18

S

schedule, 18
single parent, 7
stepbrothers, 6, 14, 18,
        20, 22
stepfather, 6, 10

stepmother, 6, 10
stepparent, 10, 12, 14,
        18, 20, 22
stepsisters, 6, 14, 18,
        20, 22

T

time, 14
traditions, 19, 22

W

wedding, 12

Websites

Due to the changing nature of Internet links, PowerKids Press has developed an online list of websites related to the subject of this book. This site is updated regularly. Please use this link to access the list: www.powerkidslinks.com/help/blended